BIBLE KEYWORDING GUIDE

beyondthehighlighter.com

MEANINGFUL MARKS WORKSHOP

EASY   ENGAGING   EXACT

Copyright © 2024 by Rob Sinclair (Beyond the Highlighter)

IT IS ILLEGAL AND UNETHICAL TO DUPLICATE COPYRIGHTED MATERIAL.

All rights reserved. No part of this publication may be reproduced, stored in a retrieval system or transmitted in any form or by any means - electronic, mechanical, photo-copy, recording, or any other – except for brief quotations in printed reviews, without the prior permission of the publisher.

Bible Keywording Guide logo mark designed by Evangela Creative
Cover design by Kristin Arbuckle
Cover photo by Mathieu / ontheroadstock@gmail.com
Edited by Tara Atterberry

Published by KAIO Publications, Inc.
www.kaiopublications.org

Scripture quotations taken from the New American Standard Bible® (NASB),
Copyright © 1960, 1962, 1963, 1968, 1971, 1972, 1973,
1975, 1977, 1995, 2020 by The Lockman Foundation
Used by permission. www.lockman.org

ISBN-13: 9781952955471

Printed in the United States of America

BIBLE STUDIES THAT HIT THE MARK.

MORE KEYWORDING GUIDES AVAILABLE AT:

CONTENTS

INTRODUCTION 1
1 THESSALONIANS 9
  STUDYING 1 THESSALONIANS 10
  GENERAL INFORMATION 11
  KEY CONCEPTS 12
  KEY WORDS 17
    BRETHREN 19
    ENCOURAGE 23
    LOVE 27
    FAITH 31
    KNOW 35
    HOLY 39
    WORD 43
    WORK 49
    AFFLICTION 53
  OPTIONAL WORDS 57
  KEY CONCLUSIONS 59
  MY KEY WORDS 60

2 THESSALONIANS ... 63
STUDYING 2 THESSALONIANS ... 64
GENERAL INFORMATION ... 65
KEY CONCEPTS ... 66
KEY WORDS ... 73
BRETHREN ... 75
LOVE ... 79
FAITH ... 81
GLORY ... 85
WORD ... 87
WORK ... 91
AFFLICTION ... 95
OPTIONAL WORDS ... 97
KEY CONCLUSIONS ... 98
MY KEY WORDS ... 99

BIBLE KEYWORDING GUIDE
Beyond the Highlighter

1 & 2 THESSALONIANS

ROB SINCLAIR

INTRODUCTION
BEYOND THE HIGHLIGHTER

As a preacher, I am regularly asked, "I have read the Bible cover to cover several times; what do I do next?" Maybe you have asked something similar regarding your own Bible study and have felt disengaged from God's Word. My answer is to study a Bible book more in depth than you've ever thought possible...and make it look easy with the *Bible Keywording Guide*.

The *Bible Keywording Guide* (BKG) is an easy-to-use series of manuals designed to help Bible students of any level identify and mark critical information found in each book of the Bible. This includes things like: key words, purpose statements, prayers, etc. Each Bible book has its own set of peculiarities that, when marked, help the reader understand what the author is really saying.

I was told once by a friend that before he understood what keywording was, a mechanical pencil and a yellow highlighter were "standard procedure" when it came to marking important ideas and insights in his Bible. Maybe this sentiment has been true for you as well. Engage in this process and see how the *Bible Keywording Guide* will take you beyond the highlighter and bring you to a whole new level of Bible study!

THE IMPORTANCE OF KEYWORDING

WHAT IS A KEY WORD? – A key word is a word that holds a significant theological meaning and is often repeated by the author to convey his points and purposes for writing. Key words are related to the themes and overall scope of the books. Without them, the author's emphasis and meanings would be greatly diminished, and even nonexistent in many cases. Keywording is an essential component of Bible study (i.e. exegesis) and is done using colors and/or symbols to distinguish certain words in the text. Leave the highlighter in the drawer...you're using a dynamic and multicolored system now!

FREQUENCY – Some key words are used a lot; others are used less frequently. If a writer uses a word consistently – repeating it over and over – then that word is a key word. Sometimes, however, key words are used less frequently and may not be as noticeable, purely based on quantity. Words like *of* and *the* would not be considered key words, even though they are some of the most frequently used words in the Bible. On the other hand, some words are extremely theologically charged, but aren't used much. For example, *wisdom* (*sophia*) is a very important and theologically significant word in the book of James, but it is only used five times in the letter.

WORD FAMILIES – Word families are filtered in the BKG to make keywording even easier. Root words and lemmas will be distinguished in this guide with an *R* or *L*. A root word (*R*) is a word that encompasses an entire family of words joined together by the same stem, whereas a lemma (*L*) is a specific word within that root's family. This distinction is made in the BKG due to the fact that sometimes an entire family of words helps the reader understand how the writer is developing a particular concept. On the other hand, sometimes only a particular word within that larger word family is theologically significant. An excellent example to distinguish the importance of these elements would be the root word, *kaleō*, which means "to call" or "to invite." Words like *parakaleō* (*comfort/urge*), *paraklēsis* (*exhort*), and *ekklēsia* (*church/assembly*) are all lemma forms of the root word *kaleō*. If the key word to be marked is *ekklēsia*, then there is no need to mark all forms of its root word, *kaleō*.

CHAPTER-SPECIFIC KEY WORDS – Most key words in a Bible book are used throughout the entire work, but some only make a strong appearance in a chapter or two. Consider *wisdom* (*sophia*) again. Of its 28 uses in 1 Corinthians, *wisdom* appears 26 times in the first three chapters. The idea may be present in other parts of the book, but the word itself doesn't make much of an appearance elsewhere. Just because a word makes a strong showing for a few chapters, and then very little afterwards, does not mean it isn't a key word. Chapter-specific key words must still be considered because of their theological contributions to their books.

OPTIONAL WORDS – Most of these guides will contain an "Optional Words" list. Optional Words will be those words that are of some interest, but may not be used for a few different reasons: (1) they may not be exceedingly theologically significant, (2) they may be used so frequently that to mark them would mean making your Bible pages extremely crowded or too busy to focus on the other words marked, or (3) they may just be synonyms to the key words. It will be at the user's discretion whether or not to mark these words. In cases where references for these words are not provided, a Biblical concordance will help you identify their uses if you choose to mark them.

KEY CONCEPTS

The BKG will also assist you in the identification and marking of other important exegetical/Bible study elements when available. For instance, the New Testament epistles will contain things like purpose statements, prayers, and petition verbs. (Don't worry; we'll get into that later!) Many books in the Old Testament will have important textual markers and key phrases that should be marked to better understand the thought and flow of the book. With these guides, you won't miss a thing!

When available, dates of books, authors, genres, places of writing, recipients of the book, occasion of the book, etc. will be included to assist you in the study process. These elements help to form the context of each book and should be generally understood as you begin marking your Bible.

WHY YOU SHOULD KEYWORD YOUR BIBLE

SIMPLICITY – The BKG will give you a comprehensive list of all the key words in each book you're studying. You won't have to waste any time trying to determine which words and concepts you should be focusing on.

EMPHASIS ON ORIGINAL LANGUAGES – Not only will you have a complete list of key words, but you will know where those words occur in the *original language*. THIS IS THE HEART AND SOUL OF KEYWORDING! **HERE'S WHY:**

Some key words are translated differently in English while the original language never changes. A good example is the word *faith*. In many New Testament books, *faith* (*pisteuō*) is also translated as "believe," "entrusted," "sure," etc., but it remains the same Greek word. An untrained eye will miss these instances, but the BKG eliminates the possibility of overlooking or missing a key word in literal translations because of its emphasis on the original languages. Why settle for a method that only teaches you to look for certain English words when the BKG streamlines the process in the author's original language?

It's also important to realize that some words in English Bibles are not always identical in meaning. One of the best examples of this would be the word *love* in John 21:15-17. The first two times Jesus asks Peter if he loves Him, Jesus says, "Do you love (*agapaō*) Me?" to which Peter replies, "Yes, Lord; You know that I love (*phileō*) You." If the reader is not careful, he will have missed the fact that the Greek word for *love* changed a few times in this passage, thinking that the same idea for love was present for this entire encounter. The BKG will help identify these types of occurrences so that the true meaning of the text will be revealed.

NOTE: While keywording passages using this guide, you may realize that you will skip over the English word several times without marking it. Don't be alarmed! This simply means that the word, although translated in English, is not the Greek, Hebrew, or Aramaic word you are supposed to mark. Again, if you mark every occurrence of *love* the same way, you will accidentally equate *agapaō* and *phileō*. However, this should not discourage you from marking synonyms in the text if they are indeed synonyms.

FASTER AND EASIER STUDY – Once your Bible is marked, you will immediately notice the important things next time you open it to study. Do you want to study *suffering* in 1 Peter or show someone how James writes about *wisdom*? Just turn there in your marked Bible and you will see these concepts fly off the page! You won't have to spend precious time scanning paragraph after paragraph for specific words or concepts anymore. Plus, you'll notice how all of those verses are related to one another instantly!

YOUR BIBLE WILL BE BEAUTIFUL – There's something incredibly satisfying about looking down at a freshly marked page of the Bible. Not only will it give you an amazing sense of accomplishment, it could very well inspire your friends and family to study God's Word with you! Marked Bibles tend to be eye-catching and often spark interest in others.

CUSTOMIZE: MAKE YOUR MARK

COMPLETE CUSTOMIZATION – One of the many advantages of the BKG is that it allows for complete customization. Suggestions for colors and symbols will be provided throughout the guides, but you can always decide (and design) for yourself which symbol or mark you'd rather use in the "My Mark" sections. If you just hate the color orange, mix it up and develop your own color system! The suggestions given generally follow a certain pattern (i.e. red is usually used for negative things – yellow is generally used for bright things, etc.). If you don't want to mark one of the key words for whatever reason, simply leave the "Marked" box unchecked for future reference.

"MY KEY WORDS" – If you find some words during your study that you believe are key to the text but are not listed in the guide, add them to the "My Key Words" section toward the back. Fill in the information for these words and design your own symbol for them!

DO SOME COLORFUL RESEARCH – Before you begin marking your Bible, do some research and determine which markers, pens, or pencils suit *your* needs and *your* Bible the best. Some Bible pages are too thin to handle certain brands of markers, and the markers bleed through very easily. Even if a brand of markers is marketed as Bible friendly, caution and experimentation should be used prior to commitment. Feel free to use a combination of these writing utensils. I personally enjoy using colored pencils because they never bleed through, rarely fade, are cost effective, and are standardized in color within their brands.

NOTE: Make sure you have a ruler or other straight edge available when marking straight lines. Squiggly lines made by freehand can look messy!

CHOOSE YOUR LITERAL TRANSLATION

THE BKG IS COMPATIBLE WITH LITERAL TRANSLATIONS OF THE BIBLE – Scriptures in the BKG come from the *New American Standard Bible* (NASB), 1995 update. This translation was chosen for these guides because it remains one of the smoothest and yet most literal translations available on today's market. Other recommended translations to accompany this guide would be the *English Standard Version* (ESV), the *New King James Version* (NKJV), the *King James Version* (KJV), or the *Revised Standard Version* (RSV). Even though the English key words will differ in these translations on occasion (e.g. *brethren* vs. *brothers*), it is still very easy to understand which word should be keyworded to the original languages using this guide.

NOTE: Wide margin Bibles are ideal for keywording! With the amount of marking, underlining, list making, etc. it will be more convenient to have some margin space to play with.

NOTE: On extremely rare occasions it will look like a word is missing in some of the Key Word tables, having been replaced with a (•). Don't worry! This simply means that on this uncommon occasion, the translators are telling us that the original word is there, but is very cumbersome to translate and make it make sense in English given the grammar of the rest of the sentence. Mark these instances as well and know that the meaning of the verse hasn't been changed, but the insertion of the word would make the sentence too awkward in English.

PARAPHRASES AND KEYWORDING – Literal translations are essential to effective keywording. In fact, it is not possible to keyword paraphrased versions like *The Message* because they are not based on the original languages. These versions are more concerned with concepts and not the actual words of the original text.

DYNAMIC EQUIVALENCY AND KEYWORDING – It is possible to keyword translations like the *New Living Translation* (NLT) and the *New International Version* (NIV), but it is not recommended. Translations such as these were translated using the Dynamic Equivalency method, which does not highly emphasize the original languages and sacrifices literality for readability. This is seen very clearly in that the NLT and NIV sometimes translate one Greek word upwards of ten different ways in English to help the reader understand the meaning. However, the meaning actually becomes less clear with every additional word—which many times isn't even synonymous—used in place of the original word.

THE USER SHOULD NOTE that keywording the Biblical text is only one part in the study process. It is not the purpose of the BKG to identify *ALL* important elements in a text, but rather to aid in the identification of key words that may go unseen in English translations.

Certain additional facts and elements will be provided when warranted, but will not be exhaustive. Things such as places, expressions of time, lists, comparisons, contrasts, causes and effects, figures of speech, important conjunctions, verbs, pronouns, etc. will be identified at times, but not extensively since they can be identified in English. However, after the text is keyworded, finding most of these other things will be much easier.

"For this reason we also constantly thank God that when you received the word of God which you heard from us, you accepted it not as the word of men, but for what it really is, the word of God, which also performs its work in you who believe."

1 Thessalonians 2:13

1 THESSALONIANS

STUDYING 1 THESSALONIANS

1. Read the introduction to one of these guides at least once.
2. Read Acts 16:1-17:15 to understand the background of the Thessalonian church.
3. Read the "General Information" page to orient yourself to 1 Thessalonians.
4. Read 1 Thessalonians all the way through several times to familiarize yourself with the text.
5. Follow the directions found under "Key Concepts." This section will have you mark other important things prior to keywording the book.
6. Keyword the book:
    a. Turn to the first keywording page (e.g. *Brethren*) and locate the suggested symbol for that particular word.
    b. Use the reference list provided in order to locate the English words in your Bible that correspond to their respective Greek word.
    c. Mark the located word with the suggested symbol. Do this for all the key words provided in each guide.
    d. When applicable, answer the questions and/or follow the study prompts included for the words.
    e. For an even deeper study of the word, define it using a reputable Bible dictionary.
7. Mark the optional words at your own discretion using the suggested symbols or by creating your own.
8. Complete the "Key Conclusions" section.
9. Utilize the "My Key Words" section when applicable.

GENERAL INFORMATION

AUTHOR	PAUL THE APOSTLE
GENRE	EPISTLE
DATE	c. 51 A.D.
WRITTEN FR.	CORINTH (cf. Acts 18:1-11; 1 Thess. 1:1)
RECIPIENTS	TO THE CHURCH OF THE THESSALONIANS (1:1)

Former Jews	Acts 17:1-4
God-fearing Greeks	Acts 17:4
Leading Women	Acts 17:4
Pagan Idolaters	1 Thess. 1:9

OCCASION

Paul and his companions were only able to proclaim the Gospel in Thessalonica for three weeks before being run out of town by the Jews, who became jealous of the peoples' response to the Word (Acts 17:1-10). Knowing that the Thessalonians' faith was in jeopardy because of these circumstances, Paul desperately sought to make it back to them to "complete what was lacking in their faith" (1 Thess. 3:10). Not being able to visit them himself, Paul sent Timothy to check on them. It was when Timothy brought back a good report about this young church (1 Thess. 3:6) that Paul sat down and penned the letter known as 1 Thessalonians.

KEY CONCEPTS

PURPOSE STATEMENT

Although Paul does not use his typical phrases: "I write to you because" or "I have written", his purpose for writing to the Thessalonians shines through his desire to make it back to them quickly. He is anxious to return to this young, persecuted church in order that he may "complete what is lacking in [their] your faith" (3:10). Recall the events of Acts 17:1-15, which tells us that Paul and his fellow workers could not stay in Thessalonica as long as they needed after urgently fleeing the riotous mob that was pursuing them. As you read this letter from Paul, keep his purpose for writing in mind and take note of how other things he mentions relate back to his statement in 3:10.

"...as we night and day keep praying most earnestly that we may see your face, and may complete what is lacking in your faith" – 1 Thessalonians 3:10

Suggestion: Lightly underline this verse using a distinct color. (Orange?)

Marked: ☐ | My Mark:

Notes:

PRAYERS

It's important to identify when a writer prays about something pertaining to his audience. Prayers tell us what else is heavy upon the writer's mind, and in many cases, can serve as secondary purpose statements. In 1 Thessalonians 1:2-5, Paul speaks of how often he remembers the Thessalonians in his prayers and thanks God for their strong faith. Paul's prayer in 3:9-13 includes his overall purpose—to make it back to the Thessalonians to complete their faith—and his beseeching of God to establish them more fervently. In 5:23, Paul uses his standard prayer terminology by starting off with "Now may..." and expresses his desire for the Thessalonians to be sanctified to God. Start a list below or in your Bible's margins that details all of the things Paul desires in praying for the Thessalonians when you get to each individual prayer. 2 Thessalonians will have some prayers you may want to add to this list.

Prayer of Remembrance	1 Thessalonians 1:2-5
Prayer of Completion	1 Thessalonians 3:9-13
Prayer for Sanctification	1 Thessalonians 5:23

Suggestion: Lightly underline these prayers using a distinct color. (Purple?)

Note: 3:10 may already be marked as the purpose statement. You can either double up the underline in verse 10 or skip from verse 9 to 11.

Marked: ☐   **My Mark:**

Notes:

PETITION VERBS

Petition verbs are a writer's way of emphasizing important points. Just like we might use an exclamation point or a bold font today, Biblical writers used petition verbs. In the verses below, Paul is urging the Thessalonians to focus and pay attention to the points connected to these verbs. If you'd like, make a list of the things Paul is urging the Thessalonians to do as you come to each verb.

Note: These verbs are in the context of Paul emphasizing important issues to which the Thessalonians should take heed. The petition verb, *parakaleō*, is also a key word for 1 Thessalonians; therefore, don't be confused when Paul uses the word in other contexts (see *Encourage* – note the overlap of uses in 4:1, 10; 5:14).

PETITION VERBS	REFERENCE	GREEK	TRANSLITERATION
IMPLORE	2:11	μαρτύρομαι	*martyromai*
EXHORT	4:1	παρακαλέω	*parakaleō*
SOLEMNLY WARN	4:6	διαμαρτύρομαι	*diamartyromai*
COMMAND	4:11	παραγγέλλω	*parangellō*
REQUEST	4:1 5:12	ἐρωτάω	*erōtaō*
URGE	4:10 5:14	παρακαλέω	*parakaleō*
ADJURE	5:27	ἐνορκίζω	*enorkizō*

Suggestion: Mark these words with a distinct symbol. (↑ ?)
You may also choose to underline the entire verse.

Marked: ☐   My Mark:

Notes:

THE COMING OF THE LORD

Jesus' second coming is the most recurring theme throughout Paul's two letters to Thessalonica. Seven of the eight chapters that comprise 1 & 2 Thessalonians make mention of the Lord's coming (*parousia*), illustrating why it should be considered a key concept. Paul evidently spent a lot of time teaching these young Christians about this event and made great efforts to keep them from misunderstanding how the second coming of Christ would occur. Notice that by the time Paul writes his second letter to this church that some individual(s) made attempts to "deceive" them in this matter, either by a spirit (false prophecy), a message (spoken word), or a letter, as if it was written by Paul himself (2 Thess. 2:2-3). But Paul won't let whoever this is get away with it – giving clear evidence that the Lord has not yet returned and that both living and deceased Christians have the ultimate hope of being with God forever.

"wait for His Son from heaven"	1 Thessalonians 1:10
"in the presence of our Lord Jesus at His coming"	1 Thessalonians 2:19
"at the coming of our Lord Jesus with all His saints"	1 Thessalonians 3:13
DETAILED DESCRIPTION OF JESUS' COMING	1 Thessalonians 4:13-5:11
"without blame at the coming of our Lord Jesus Christ."	1 Thessalonians 5:23
DETAILED DESCRIPTION OF JESUS' COMING	2 Thessalonians 1:7-10
DETAILED DESCRIPTION OF JESUS' COMING	2 Thessalonians 2:1-3

Suggestion: Draw a symbol in the margin of these verses / passages. (⬇?)
If you'd rather, simply mark every use of "coming" or "comes" as it pertains to Jesus' return with this same symbol in the passages listed above.

Note: Not every use of "coming," "comes," or "came" has reference to Jesus' coming, so be careful of the context before marking.

Marked: ☐   **My Mark:**

Study:

🔍 Notice the sequence of events that Paul gives and the nature of the second coming of Christ in 4:13-5:11. Record your observations regarding the progression of this *coming*.

KEY WORDS

BRETHREN

It's an amazing thing that a person can be a pagan idolater one moment, and then submit his life to the Lord and be counted among His chosen the next. Those who responded to the Gospel in Thessalonica were an eclectic group. Jews, pagans, God-fearing Greeks, and leading women are said to have been persuaded by the message in Acts 17:4 (cf. 1 Thess. 1:9). This diverse group of people are now *brethren*. They are all part of the body of Christ, sharing a common salvation with Christians around the world. Unity and camaraderie are tremendous blessings of the church, and these young, persecuted Christians will need one another from the very first day they proclaimed Jesus as Lord, rather than Caesar.

WORD	GREEK-R	TRANSLITERATION	OCCURRENCES	SUGGESTED SYMBOL
Brethren	ἀδελφός	*adelphos*	20	Brethren

Marked: ☐   **My Mark:**

1 Thess. 1:4	knowing,	brethren	beloved by God, *His* choice of you;
1 Thess. 2:1	For you yourselves know,	brethren	, that our coming to you was not
1 Thess. 2:9	For you recall,	brethren	, our labor and hardship, *how*
1 Thess. 2:14	For you,	brethren	, became imitators of the churches
1 Thess. 2:17	But we,	brethren	, having been taken away from you
1 Thess. 3:2	and we sent Timothy, our	brother	and God's fellow worker in the
1 Thess. 3:7	for this reason,	brethren	, in all our distress and
1 Thess. 4:1	Finally then,	brethren	, we request and exhort you in the
1 Thess. 4:6	man transgress and defraud his	brother	in the matter because the Lord is
1 Thess. 4:9	as to the love of the	brethren	, you have no need
1 Thess. 4:10	you do practice it toward all the	brethren	who are in all Macedonia. But we
1 Thess. 4:10	all Macedonia. But we urge you,	brethren	, to excel still more,
1 Thess. 4:13	not want you to be uninformed,	brethren	, about those who are asleep, so
1 Thess. 5:1	as to the times and the epochs,	brethren	, you have no need of anything to
1 Thess. 5:4	But you,	brethren	, are not in darkness, that the
1 Thess. 5:12	But we request of you,	brethren	, that you appreciate those who
1 Thess. 5:14	We urge you,	brethren	, admonish the unruly, encourage

1 Thess. 5:25		Brethren, pray for us.
1 Thess. 5:26	Greet all the	brethren with a holy kiss.
1 Thess. 5:27	have this letter read to all the	brethren.

Study:

- 🔍 Paul makes a beautiful connection between his calling the Thessalonians *brethren* and making the point that they are now *imitators* (*mimētēs*) of their older brothers in Christ: Paul, Timothy, and Silas. If you'd like, locate and mark *imitators* (*mimētēs*) in 1:6 and 2:14 with a similarly colored symbol (see "Optional Words" for a symbol suggestion).

  Marked: ☐   **My Mark:**

- 🔍 Another closely related word to *brethren* and *imitators* is *example* (*typos*) in 1:7. Just as Paul and the other missionaries were examples to the Thessalonians, the Thessalonians themselves became examples to others and were considered worthy of *imitation* by other churches! Mark this word if you'd like in 1:7 with a similar symbol as *imitators*.

  Marked: ☐   **My Mark:**

- 🔍 Speaking of *brethren* and following *examples*, Paul points to an unfortunate necessity concerning some of the *brethren* in this new church. There are some who are *unruly* (*ataktos*) whom the leadership is charged to admonish in 5:14. This word could almost go unmarked, except for the fact that some *unruly* brethren will continue causing problems which Paul will address again in 2 Thessalonians. Mark *unruly* in 5:14 (see "Optional Words" for a symbol suggestion).

  Marked: ☐   **My Mark:**

- 🔍 Be careful not to confuse unruly / undisciplined Christians in these letters with those who are not Christians at all. Words like 'outsiders,' 'others,' and 'the rest' will be addressed later under *Affliction*.

Question:

- 📖 Why do you think Paul refers to this group of Christians as *brethren* so frequently? (See *Brethren* in 2 Thessalonians for additional thoughts).

📖 Who do you find yourself imitating in your own life? What makes that person worth imitating?

📖 Does anyone imitate your faith? Is that a good or bad thing?

Notes:

ENCOURAGE

Paul knows that without he and his missionary colleagues present, the Thessalonians will only have each other to rely on when their faith is tested. The apostle has a deep love for this tender-footed church and does not want to see their zeal for the Lord wane. There are a number of terms in 1 & 2 Thessalonians that Paul uses to emphasize the importance of Christian relationships and connection. *Brethren* is the most common term of unity (previous section), followed by *encourage/exhort* and *one another* in this section, with *love*, *thanks*, and *joy* in the next section. While marking the terms in this section, pay very close attention to how the Thessalonians are to *encourage* each other and what exactly they are to do for *one another*. The conclusion is clear. If done sincerely and often, *encouragement* from fellow Christians will have a tremendously positive impact on the spiritual lives of others. After all, what are brothers and sisters in Christ for?

WORD	GREEK-L	TRANSLITERATION	OCC...	SUGGESTED SYMBOL
Encourage	παρακαλέω	*parakaleō*	8	Encourage

Marked: ☐   My Mark:

1 Thess. 2:11	just as you know how we were	exhorting	and encouraging and imploring each
1 Thess. 3:2	of Christ, to strengthen and	encourage	you as to your faith,
1 Thess. 3:7	distress and affliction we were	comforted	about you through your faith;
1 Thess. 4:1	then, brethren, we request and	exhort	you in the Lord Jesus, that as you
1 Thess. 4:10	who are in all Macedonia. But we	urge	you, brethren, to excel still
1 Thess. 4:18	Therefore	comfort	one another with these words.
1 Thess. 5:11	Therefore	encourage	one another and build up one
1 Thess. 5:14	We	urge	you, brethren, admonish the

WORD	GREEK-L	TRANSLITERATION	OCC...	SUGGESTED SYMBOL
Encourage	παραμυθέομαι	*paramytheomai*	2	Encourage

1 Thess. 2:11	how we were exhorting and	encouraging	and imploring
1 Thess. 5:14	admonish the unruly,	encourage	the fainthearted

WORD	GREEK-L	TRANSLITERATION	OCC...	SUGGESTED SYMBOL
Exhort	παράκλησις	*paraklēsis*	1	Exhort

1 Thess. 2:3	For our	exhortation	does not *come* from error or

WORD	GREEK-L	TRANSLITERATION	OCC...	SUGGESTED SYMBOL
One Another	ἀλλήλων	*allēlōn*	5	One Another

Marked: ☐   My Mark:

1 Thess. 3:12	increase and abound in love for	one another	, and for all people, just
1 Thess. 4:9	are taught by God to love	one another	;
1 Thess. 4:18	Therefore comfort	one another	with these words.
1 Thess. 5:11	Therefore encourage	one another	and build up one another,
1 Thess. 5:15	seek after that which is good for	one another	and for all people.

WORD	GREEK-L	TRANSLITERATION	OCC...	SUGGESTED SYMBOL
One Another	ἑαυτοῦ	*heautou*	1	One Another

1 Thess. 5:13	of their work. Live in peace with	one another	.

WORD	GREEK-L	TRANSLITERATION	OCC...	SUGGESTED SYMBOL
One Another	εἷς	*heis*	1	One Another

1 Thess. 5:11	one another and build up	one another	, just as you also are

WORD	GREEK-L	TRANSLITERATION	OCCURRENCES	SUGGESTED SYMBOL
Another	τὶς	*tis*	1	Another

1 Thess. 5:15	See that no one repays	another	with evil for evil, but always

Study:

🔍 Look for *one another* in 2 Thessalonians 1:3 and mark it with the same symbol.

Marked: ☐   My Mark:

🔍 A synonymous term to mark in conjunction with *encourage* and *one another* is 'build up' (*oikodomeō*) in 5:11. Mark it with the same symbol as *encourage* if you'd like. For now, wait to mark the other words that have to do with *encourage* and *one another* (like *love*, *strengthen*, *excel*, etc.), since they'll have their own suggested symbols later.

Marked: ☐   My Mark:

🔍 Look up the definition of 'build up' (*oikodomeō*) in your Bible dictionary. How does this word expand your understanding of what the Thessalonians were to do for one another?

Definition of 'build up' (*oikodomeō*):

🔍 Make a list of all the things Paul instructed the Thessalonians to do for *one another* and ways they were to *encourage* each other.

The Thessalonians were to:

Question:

📖 Given what you know about the history of the establishment of the church in Thessalonica (Acts 17:1-15), why do you think Paul spoke of *encouragement* so much?

📖 Go back and read 2 Thessalonians 1:3 since you have already marked *one another* in that passage. What does *one another* in this verse tell us about the Christians in Thessalonica? Why do you think that is the case?

📖 What do you think are some of the best ways to *encourage* your fellow Christians?

📖 Do you find it easy to be *encouraging* to others? Why or why not?

📖 List at least one thing you can do today that will *encourage* a fellow Christian. How do you think they will respond if you act on this?

Notes:

LOVE

Although there are three different words for *love* used in the New Testament Scriptures, Paul emphasizes *agapē* love in his letters to Thessalonica. This kind of love prioritizes others above self and seeks to fulfill the best interests of others, even at the risk of personal sacrifice. Paul and company embodied this sort of love when they came to Thessalonica to preach the Gospel in the first place, knowing that persecutions likely awaited them. He said in 1 Thess. 2:2, "but after we had already suffered and been mistreated in Philippi, as you know, we had the boldness in our God to speak to you the Gospel of God amid much opposition." The Gospel of Jesus Christ had to make it to Thessalonica, no matter what the cost. It should not surprise us that Paul speaks of *love* so much in 1 Thessalonians since we have already seen how many relational terms he has used, such as *brethren, encourage, one another*, etc. A special note will be made in this section regarding the terms, *joy* and *thanks* as well.

WORD	GREEK-R	TRANSLITERATION	OCCURRENCES	SUGGESTED SYMBOL
Love	αγαπαω	*agapaō*	8	L♥ve

Marked: ☐   **My Mark:**

1 Thess. 1:3	your work of faith and labor of	love	and steadfastness of hope in our
1 Thess. 1:4	knowing, brethren	beloved	by God, *His* choice of you;
1 Thess. 2:8	because you had become	very dear	to us.
1 Thess. 3:6	us good news of your faith and	love	, and that you always think kindly
1 Thess. 3:12	you to increase and abound in	love	for one another, and for all
1 Thess. 4:9	yourselves are taught by God to	love	one another;
1 Thess. 5:8	on the breastplate of faith and	love	, and as a helmet, the hope of
1 Thess. 5:13	esteem them very highly in	love	because of their work. Live in

Study:

🔍 You probably noticed in 4:9 that you only marked one word for love, even though there were two. The reason for this is that the phrase, *love of the brethren*, is actually the Greek word *philadelphia*, not *agapaō*. Recall that the word for *brethren* is *adelphos*, which is part of the word *philadelphia*. You already marked it! If you'd like, look up each of these words in a Bible dictionary and compare them.

Definition of *love* (*agapao*):

Definition of *love* (*philadelphia*):

🔍 The Thessalonians have accepted the Word of the Lord with *joy* (*chara*), and Paul *rejoices* (*chairō*) over them because of their response, writing to them that they are his hope, glory, and joy (2:19-20). This young church at Thessalonica is not without its problems, but Paul still loves them greatly and writes of his *joy* in regard to them six times in this five-chapter book. If you'd like, mark the references to *joy* and *rejoice*. (See "Optional Words" for a symbol suggestion.)

Joy (*chara*): 1:6; 2:19, 20; 3:9

Marked: ☐   **My Mark:**

Rejoice (*chairō*): 3:9; 5:16

Marked: ☐   **My Mark:**

🔍 Every time Paul uses the word *thanks* in 1 Thessalonians, it is gratitude toward God for His work in the lives of these believers. The apostle is under no delusion that the Thessalonians believe solely because of him. It is because of the Gospel and their secure salvation brings Paul great *joy*. Witnessing a group of people receive the Word of God in such circumstances and remain faithful is a great encouragement to him. I was once thanked by the man who helped bring me to Christ. He told me it was such a relief to know that at least one person to which he taught the Gospel would remain faithful. Perhaps this is how Paul felt? If you'd like, mark the references to *thanks* in both 1 & 2 Thessalonians. (See "Optional Words" for a symbol suggestion).

Thanks (*eucharisteō*):   **1 Thess.:** 1:2; 2:13; 5:18 / 3:9 (*eucharistia*)

2 Thess.: 1:3; 2:13

Marked: ☐   **My Mark:**

Question:

- 📖 In 2:8, Paul says that he and his companions were "well-pleased to impart to you not only the Gospel of God but also our own lives." How would you describe what it means to impart your life to someone?

- 📖 Have you ever imparted your life to anyone and/or has anyone imparted their lives to you? What did that look like for you?

- 📖 Regarding *love*, Paul says that the Thessalonians are practicing it "toward all the brethren who are in all Macedonia" (4:10). What does it mean to "practice love" toward others?

- 📖 Consider your own relationships with fellow Christians. What about your brothers and sisters in Christ gives you great *joy*?

- 📖 Paul said that he "constantly" and "always" thanked God for the Thessalonians and their steadfast faith. How often do you *thank* God for your Christian brothers and sisters? If you do, do you tell them? If you don't, why not?

Notes:

FAITH

While *brethren* stands as the frontrunning key word in these letters concerning Christians and their relationships with one another, *faith* is the predominant key word Paul uses when addressing this church's relationship with the Creator. The Thessalonians had *faith* indeed. The believing Jews embraced Jesus, the long-awaited Messiah they hoped would arrive. The idolaters turned from their lifeless objects of worship to serve a "living and true God," (1:9). The God-fearing Greeks gladly accepted the good news, even if it meant broken earthly relationships. This group was all in – having totally rerouted their lives for Jesus' sake. Paul recognizes the great efforts this congregation was making, calling to mind their "work of *faith* and labor of *love*" (1:3). They owned it. Notice that Paul constantly writes about "*Your* faith" – "*You* who believe" – "*Your* work of faith." Their faith was so evident that everyone who encountered the Thessalonian Christians reported their newfound trust in God to others (1:7-9).

WORD	GREEK-R	TRANSLITERATION	OCCURRENCES	SUGGESTED SYMBOL
Faith	πιστευω	*pisteuō*	14	Faith

Marked: ☐   **My Mark:**

1 Thess. 1:3	bearing in mind your work of	faith	and labor of love and
1 Thess. 1:7	you became an example to all the	believers	in Macedonia and in Achaia.
1 Thess. 1:8	but also in every place your	faith	toward God has gone forth, so
1 Thess. 2:4	have been approved by God to be	entrusted	with the gospel, so we speak, not
1 Thess. 2:10	blamelessly we behaved toward you	believers	;
1 Thess. 2:13	also performs its work in you who	believe	.
1 Thess. 3:2	and encourage you as to your	faith	,
1 Thess. 3:5	also sent to find out about your	faith	, for fear that the tempter might
1 Thess. 3:6	has brought us good news of your	faith	and love, and that you always
1 Thess. 3:7	comforted about you through your	faith	;
1 Thess. 3:10	complete what is lacking in your	faith	?
1 Thess. 4:14	For if we	believe	that Jesus died and rose again,
1 Thess. 5:8	having put on the breastplate of	faith	and love, and as a helmet, the
1 Thess. 5:24		Faithful	is He who calls you, and He also

WORD	GREEK-R	TRANSLITERATION	OCCURRENCES	SUGGESTED SYMBOL
Hope	ελπις	*elpis*	4	Hope

Marked: ☐ **My Mark:**

1 Thess. 1:3	of love and steadfastness of	hope	in our Lord Jesus Christ in the
1 Thess. 2:19	For who is our	hope	or joy or crown of exultation? Is
1 Thess. 4:13	grieve as do the rest who have no	hope	.
1 Thess. 5:8	and love, and as a helmet, the	hope	of salvation.

Study:

🔍 *Faith (pisteuō) and hope (elpis) are the most recurring words (by root) in 1 & 2 Thessalonians; these highlight the transcendent Christian anticipation of eternal life in the presence of God. However, there are an abundance of other 'faith words' in these letters that Paul implements to keep these Christians motivated. There are too many to list as "Optional Words," so a starter list is provided below. You may find other words you'll want to add, so space is provided below the list.* (**Suggestion:** Put a green box around these words and phrases).

Note: 2 Thessalonians will have a similar list under the 'Faith' section.

Steadfastness	(*hupomonē*)	1:3
Strengthen	(*stērizō*)	3:2, 13 (establish)
Stand Firm	(*stēkō*)	3:8
Alert	(*grēgoreō*)	5:6, 10
Sober	(*nēphō*)	5:6, 8
Breastplate	(*thōrax*)	5:8
Helmet	(*perikephalaia*)	5:8
Hold Fast	(*katechō*)	5:21

Marked: ☐ **My Mark:**

Question:

📖 Paul praises the Thessalonians very highly for their tremendous *faith*, but he still says he desires to see them face-to-face in order to "complete what is lacking" in their faith (3:10). What do you suppose Paul wanted to "complete" regarding this congregation's faith? (See Chapters 4-5 for some ideas)

📖 What are some characteristics that stand out to you about the Thessalonians' faith?

📖 What has their faith accomplished?

📖 Do you think your faith could accomplish the same things? Why or why not?

📖 Paul mentions a group that he calls, "the rest" in 4:13, and says they "have no hope." Does this mean that some people just can't be saved? What might be some reasons why some "have no hope"? (cf. 2 Thessalonians 3:1-2)

Notes:

KNOW

Paul explained to the Roman congregation that "...faith comes from hearing, and hearing by the word of Christ" (Rom. 10:17). The Thessalonians came by their faith in Jesus by listening to Paul and coming to *know* who the Lord is. Look back at Acts 17:1-4, when Paul met the Thessalonians and began presenting Christ to them. In verses 2-3, it's said that Paul reasoned (*dialegomai*) with them from the Scriptures, explained (*dianoigō*) and gave evidence (*paratithēmi*) regarding Jesus and His anointing as the Christ. These believers know who Jesus is and have chosen to have a relationship with their Creator. Paul undoubtedly spent his three weeks in Thessalonica continuing to reason, explain, and give evidence to anyone who would listen. Notice that the apostle writes to the Thessalonians as if they *currently* know these things and not as if they need to come to know them. This group *knows* what they need to know, and must "examine everything carefully" (5:21) when presented with information that challenges what they know to be true.

WORD	GREEK-R	TRANSLITERATION	OCCURRENCES	SUGGESTED SYMBOL
Know	οιδα	*oida*	13	Know

Marked: ☐

My Mark:

1 Thess. 1:4		knowing	, brethren beloved by God, *His*
1 Thess. 1:5	with full conviction; just as you	know	what kind of men we proved to be
1 Thess. 2:1	For you yourselves	know	, brethren, that our coming to you
1 Thess. 2:2	mistreated in Philippi, as you	know	, we had the boldness in our God
1 Thess. 2:5	with flattering speech, as you	know	, nor with a pretext for greed—God
1 Thess. 2:11	just as you	know	how we *were* exhorting and
1 Thess. 3:3	afflictions; for you yourselves	know	that we have been destined for
1 Thess. 3:4	and so it came to pass, as you	know	.
1 Thess. 4:2	For you	know	what commandments we gave you by
1 Thess. 4:4	that each of you	know	how to possess his own vessel in
1 Thess. 4:5	like the Gentiles who do not	know	God;
1 Thess. 5:2	For you yourselves	know	full well that the day of the Lord
1 Thess. 5:12	of you, brethren, that you	appreciate	those who diligently labor among

Study:

🔍 Paul uses other words/phrases that emphasize that the Thessalonians have the *knowledge* they need to live faithful lives for Christ. If you'd like, mark "recall" (2:9), "witnesses" (2:10), and "kept telling you" (3:4) with the same symbol you used for *know*, since they are contextually related to Paul's phrase "you know" in other passages.

Marked: ☐   **My Mark:**

🔍 Paul continues reassuring this congregation in 2 Thessalonians that they have the true knowledge of God and need not worry about false information presented by impostors. You may also want to mark *know* in 2 Thessalonians 1:8, 2:6, and 3:7 with the same symbol you used for 1 Thessalonians. Also note that there are other words/phrases that denote the same thing as *knowledge* in that letter. For instance, you may wish to mark "remember" and "I was telling you these things" in 2 Thess. 2:5.

Marked: ☐   **My Mark:**

🔍 Revisit Acts 17:2-3 again and consider the ways in which Paul imparted the *knowledge* of Jesus to the Thessalonians. Look up the words *reasoned* (*dialegomai*), *explaining* (*dianoigō*), and *evidence* (*paratithēmi*) in your Bible dictionary and compare their definitions.

Definition of *reasoned* (*dialegomai*):

Definition of *explaining* (*dianoigō*):

Definition of *evidence* (*paratithēmi*):

Question:

📖 Regarding the definitions above, how would you summarize the way Paul presented Jesus to the Thessalonians? How can you implement these same methods in your own presentation of Christ to others?

📖 *Know* (*oida*) is the root word for "appreciate" in 1 Thessalonians 5:12, regarding the leaders of the Thessalonian congregation. With that information, what do you think Paul means when he tells this group to appreciate their leaders? Do you appreciate your spiritual leaders the way Paul is talking about?

📖 What are some things you see in the text that Paul tells the Thessalonians they *know*? (Make a list if you'd like). How would you describe the importance of *knowing* these things (and similar things) in relationship to the strength of an individual's faith?

📖 What are some things that can happen to an individual's *faith* if they are not stable in their *knowledge* of Christ, the Gospel, the Scriptures, etc.? (cf. 2 Thess. 2:1-3; Gal. 1:6-10; 2 Peter 3:14-16).

Notes:

HOLY

In a fallen world, distinctiveness as God's people is a daily challenge. The Thessalonians emerged from the waters of baptism as God's people – His *holy*, set-apart people. But they, like us, still lived among the darkness and depravity of a lost world. Now free from sin, they are tasked to live differently than their idolatrous neighbors. Having received the gift of the *Holy* Spirit, Paul tells this group that, "this is the will of God, your *sanctification*" (4:3). Godly living should now characterize every thought, word, and action of these new believers. Obviously, this does not mean instant perfection, but an earnest attempt to live like Christ. Since *holy* living is the standard, Paul exhorts this group to *excel* in all areas of their faith. There is always room for improvement when striving to follow the example of Christ. Paul's emphasis on this aspect of the Thessalonians' Christianity demonstrates for us that this is a continual and sometimes difficult process because of our sins. Luckily for us, our *holiness* depends not on ourselves, but on the most holy God.

WORD	GREEK-R	TRANSLITERATION	OCCURRENCES	SUGGESTED SYMBOL
Holy	ἅγιος	*hagios*	10	Holy

Marked: ☐   **My Mark:**

1 Thess. 1:5	but also in power and in the	Holy	Spirit and with full conviction;
1 Thess. 1:6	tribulation with the joy of the	Holy	Spirit,
1 Thess. 3:13	your hearts without blame in	holiness	before our God and Father at the
1 Thess. 3:13	of our Lord Jesus with all His	saints	.
1 Thess. 4:3	For this is the will of God, your	sanctification	; *that is*, that you abstain from
1 Thess. 4:4	how to possess his own vessel in	sanctification	and honor,
1 Thess. 4:7	the purpose of impurity, but in	sanctification	.
1 Thess. 4:8	man but the God who gives His	Holy	Spirit to you.
1 Thess. 5:23	may the God of peace Himself	sanctify	you entirely; and may your spirit
1 Thess. 5:26	Greet all the brethren with a	holy	kiss.

WORD	GREEK-R	TRANSLITERATION	OCCURRENCES	SUGGESTED SYMBOL
Excel	περισσευω	*perisseuō*	6	Excel ↑

Marked: ☐   **My Mark:**

1 Thess. 2:17	in person, not in spirit—were	all the more	eager with great desire
1 Thess. 3:10	as we night and day keep praying	most	earnestly that we may see your
1 Thess. 3:12	Lord cause you to increase and	abound	in love for one another, and for
1 Thess. 4:1	you actually do walk), that you	excel	still more.
1 Thess. 4:10	But we urge you, brethren, to	excel	still more,
1 Thess. 5:13	and that you esteem them	very highly	in love because of their

Study:

🔍 The root term for *excel* (*perisseuō*) is included in the same section as *holy* because they both are related to maturing as God's people. *Holiness/sanctification* is a process. *Excelling* and growing as a Christian is a process. It is not enough for a Christian to simply become a Christian. Perseverance, Godly living, positive habits, etc. must all be developed to avoid complacency and instability in one's faith. Paul certainly knows this and, therefore, spurs these young, zealous Christians to become even more distinct as God's beloved people.

🔍 A host of other "growing"/"behavior" terms can be found in this letter. Paul uses them to demonstrate the necessity of growing up in Christ and being found by Him blameless at His coming; or dying faithfully and awaiting His resurrection of life. Make a list of the other terms in 1 Thessalonians that pertain to *holy* living and *excelling* – that is, growing as a Christian. **Note:** It will be up to you whether or not to mark the additional words, but be cautious about marking them since they might be key words you haven't studied yet in this guide.

Other words that denote holiness and excelling:

🔍 Although it is not used as frequently, Paul uses *hagios* in 2 Thessalonians as well. You may want to mark *saints* in 2 Thess. 1:10 and *sanctification* in 2 Thess. 2:13 with the same symbol.

Marked: ☐ | **My Mark:** |

Question:

📖 Note the different terms that share the root word for *holy*. How has seeing Paul's different uses of *holy* improved your understanding of the word?

📖 Just as God called the Thessalonians to *sanctification* (living distinctive, *holy* lives), He calls us to the same. Would you consider yourself to be living a *sanctified* life? Why or why not?

📖 The Thessalonians faced a great deal of persecution that must have made living the way that God wanted them to very difficult. What things in your own life are making it difficult to live *holy* day by day?

📖 What are some things Paul lists that he wants the Thessalonians to *excel* in?

📖 What are some other areas in which a Christian should be *excelling*? Make a list.

📖 Why is *excelling* as a Christian so important?

_____
_____

📖 Would you consider yourself to be an *excelling* Christian? Why or why not?

_____
_____

Notes:

WORD

God knew that there were souls eager to respond to the Gospel in Thessalonica. "A vision appeared to Paul in the night: a man of Macedonia was standing and appealing to him, and saying, "Come over to Macedonia and help us. When he had seen the vision, immediately we sought to go into Macedonia, concluding that God had called us to preach the Gospel to them" (Acts 16:9, 10). Paul and his companions were not disappointed. The Thessalonians eagerly received the Gospel. There were, unfortunately, some who did not receive the Word. Those who did soak it up allowed God's life changing message to transform them. Paul continually reminded them that the Gospel didn't come with "flattering speech," but with power, conviction, and the Holy Spirit (1:5). There was no denying that the genuine message of God had made it to Thessalonica. Note that in most cases, *word* and *Gospel* are synonymous with each other in this letter and have both been included in this section. *Received/accepted* are also words that indicate the Thessalonians' spiritual attitude in obeying the Gospel, and have been included as well.

WORD	GREEK-R	TRANSLITERATION	OCCURRENCES	SUGGESTED SYMBOL
Word	λεγω	*legō*	14	◁Word◁

Marked: ☐   **My Mark:**

1 Thess. 1:4	brethren beloved by God, *His*	choice	of you;
1 Thess. 1:5	our gospel did not come to you in	word	only, but also in power and in the
1 Thess. 1:6	of the Lord, having received the	word	in much tribulation with the joy
1 Thess. 1:8	For the	word	of the Lord has sounded forth from
1 Thess. 2:5	For we never came with flattering	speech	, as you know, nor with a pretext
1 Thess. 2:13	God that when you received the	word	of God which you heard from us,
1 Thess. 2:13	us, you accepted *it* not *as* the	word	of men, but *for* what it really is,
1 Thess. 2:13	but *for* what it really is, the	word	of God, which also performs its
1 Thess. 3:4	when we were with you, we *kept*	telling	you in advance that we were going
1 Thess. 4:6	all these things, just as we also	told	you before and solemnly warned
1 Thess. 4:15	For this we	say	to you by the word of the Lord,
1 Thess. 4:15	For this we say to you by the	word	of the Lord, that we who are alive
1 Thess. 4:18	comfort one another with these	words	.
1 Thess. 5:3	While they are	saying	, "Peace and safety!" then

WORD	GREEK-R	TRANSLITERATION	OCCURRENCES	SUGGESTED SYMBOL
Gospel	ευαγγελιον	*euaggelion*	7	Gospel

Marked: ☐   **My Mark:**

1 Thess 1:5	for our	gospel	did not come to you in word only,
1 Thess 2:2	in our God to speak to you the	gospel	of God amid much opposition.
1 Thess 2:4	by God to be entrusted with the	gospel	, so we speak, not as pleasing
1 Thess 2:8	to impart to you not only the	gospel	of God but also our own lives,
1 Thess 2:9	of you, we proclaimed to you the	gospel	of God.
1 Thess 3:2	and God's fellow worker in the	gospel	of Christ, to strengthen and
1 Thess 3:6	and has brought us	good news	of your faith and

WORD	GREEK-R	TRANSLITERATION	OCCURRENCES	SUGGESTED SYMBOL
Speak	λαλεω	*laleō*	4	Speak

Marked: ☐   **My Mark:**

1 Thess 1:8	that we have no need to	say	anything.
1 Thess 2:2	the boldness in our God to	speak	to you the gospel of God amid much
1 Thess 2:4	with the gospel, so we	speak	, not as pleasing men, but God who
1 Thess 2:16	hindering us from	speaking	to the Gentiles so that they may

WORD	GREEK-L	TRANSLITERATION	OCC...	SUGGESTED SYMBOL
Received	παραλαμβάνω	*paralambanō*	2	Received

Marked: ☐   **My Mark:**

1 Thess. 2:13	thank God that when you	received	the word of God which you heard
1 Thess. 4:1	in the Lord Jesus, that as you	received	from us *instruction* as to how you

WORD	GREEK-L	TRANSLITERATION	OCCURRENCES	SUGGESTED SYMBOL
Received	δέχομαι	*dechomai*	2	Received

Marked: ☐ | **My Mark:**

1 Thess. 1:6	of us and of the Lord, having	received	the word in much tribulation with
1 Thess. 2:13	which you heard from us, you	accepted	it *not as* the word of men, but *for*

Study:

- *Choice* (*eklogē*) in 1:4 is a speech-related term and is part of the word family of *legō*. Look this word up in a Bible dictionary and write down the definition. How does this help you understand how God chose us? Do you see a relationship to *gospel* in verse 5? (Cf. 2 Thess. 2:14; 1 Peter 2:9)

  Definition of *eklogē*:

- *Proclaimed* (2:9) is another speech term synonymous with *word* and *speak*, in terms of delivering the Gospel. If you'd like, mark this word with the same symbol you used for *word/speak*.

  Marked: ☐ | **My Mark:**

- After Paul and Silas are driven out of Thessalonica in Acts 17:10-12, they went to Berea and preached the Gospel there. It is said that the Bereans were more "noble-minded" than those in Thessalonica. Look up the word for "noble-minded" in your Bible dictionary. List some of the differences between how the Bereans *received* the *Gospel* and the obstinate group that rejected it in Thessalonica.

  Definition of *noble-minded* (*eugenēs*):

  The Bereans received the Word:

Question:

📖 Read Acts 16:6-10 again and note the route that God sent Paul and his companions to bring the Gospel to Macedonia. Why do you think God guided these men to Thessalonica, even though there would be much opposition?

📖 According to 1 Thessalonians 1:5, the Gospel came to Thessalonica not only with words, but with power, the Holy Spirit, and full conviction. What do you suppose Paul meant by these things, in addition to the verbal preaching of the Gospel? (cf. 2 Corinthians 12:12).

📖 Paul said in 2:5 that he and his colleagues never came with "flattering speech" to deliver the Gospel. How would you describe what flattering speech sounds like in the modern church culture of today? Do you think it's much different from back then?

📖 What are some other contrasts you see between the *Word* of God and the *word* of men in this letter? (e.g., 2:5, 6, 13, etc.). Would you consider the "words of men" as Paul describes in his letter a problem for the world today? Why or why not?

📖 According to 1:8-10, how did the *Word* of the Lord sound forth from the Thessalonians?

📖 When you present the *Gospel* to others, do they *accept/receive* it for what it is? How would you describe their reaction to hearing God's Word?

Notes:

WORK

The concept of *working* and *laboring* in both letters to the Thessalonians is multi-dimensional. When Paul and company make it to town, there is much work to do, both physically and spiritually. Paul and Silas set an example of good, old-fashioned *labor* by working for a living – likely making tents (cf. Acts 18:3), in order to not be a financial burden on these new believers. This example allows Paul to discuss at length the importance of Christians working so as not to gain the reputation as burdens on their community. Spiritually speaking, both 1 & 2 Thessalonians demonstrate a fascinating dynamic of the forces of good and evil working to gain control of the hearts and souls of humanity. God, the missionaries, spiritual leaders, and fellow churches are working together to stabilize this young congregation and ground them in their faith. On the other hand, Satan is working (2:18; 3:5) to undo every good thing this church has going for it. Watch for these dynamics as you mark the words pertaining to *work* and *labor*.

WORD	GREEK-R	TRANSLITERATION	OCCURRENCES	SUGGESTED SYMBOL
Work	εργον	*ergon*	6	Work (shovel)

Marked: ☐   **My Mark:**

1 Thess. 1:3	constantly bearing in mind your	work	of faith and labor of love and
1 Thess. 2:9	our labor and hardship, *how*	working	night and day so as not to be a
1 Thess. 2:13	is, the word of God, which also	performs its work	in you who believe.
1 Thess. 3:2	Timothy, our brother and God's	fellow worker	in the gospel of Christ, to
1 Thess. 4:11	attend to your own business and	work	with your hands, just as we
1 Thess. 5:13	highly in love because of their	work	. Live in peace with one another.

WORD	GREEK-R	TRANSLITERATION	OCCURRENCES	SUGGESTED SYMBOL
Labor	κοπτω	*koptō*	5	Labor (shovel)

Marked: ☐   **My Mark:**

1 Thess. 1:3	in mind your work of faith and	labor	of love and steadfastness of
1 Thess. 2:9	For you recall, brethren, our	labor	and hardship, *how* working

1 Thess. 2:18	more than once—and yet Satan	hindered	us.
1 Thess. 3:5	might have tempted you, and our	labor	would be in vain.
1 Thess. 5:12	that you appreciate those who	diligently labor	among you, and have charge

Study:

- 🔍 Be careful in this section not to mark "labor pains" in 5:3 – it is not the same word!

- 🔍 After you have keyworded both *work* (*ergon*) and *labor* (*koptō*), use a Bible dictionary to look these words up. Compare the two and see what you notice.

    Definition of *work* (*ergon*):

    Definition of *labor* (*koptō*):

    Comparison between *ergon* and *koptō*:

- 🔍 You may also want to define and mark *hardship* (*mochthos*) in 2:9 with a similar symbol as *work* and *labor*.

    Definition of *hardship* (*mochthos*):

Marked: ☐   **My Mark:**

- 🔍 In 1 Thess. 2:18, Paul states that "Satan hindered" the missionaries from being able to make it back to Thessalonica. Based on your studies of this letter so far, consider why Satan would actively work against Paul to prevent him from returning to these Christians. What could happen? Mark *Satan* with a distinct symbol (see "Optional Words" for a symbol suggestion). Then, if you wish, mark *tempter* and *tempted* in 3:5 with the same symbol.

Marked: ☐   **My Mark:**

Question:

📖 Paul calls Timothy "God's fellow worker in the gospel of Christ" in 3:2. What kind of *work* was Timothy doing in service to God and the Gospel at this time? What lessons can we learn from Timothy's *work*?

📖 What are some comparisons and contrasts you see between the *labor* of God, Paul, and the leaders of the congregation, versus the *work* of Satan in the spiritual war for these young Christians' souls?

📖 In 2:13, Paul gives thanks for the way the Thessalonians received the Word of God and states that the Word "performs its work in you who believe." Based on the definitions above and the overall context of Paul's encouraging words to these Christians, what do you think it means that the Word "performs its work" in those who believe?

Notes:

AFFLICTION

Paul, Silas, and Timothy were no strangers to affliction by the time they made it to Thessalonica. This is no surprise, given that God Himself stated in Acts 9:16 that Paul would suffer for His name's sake in bringing the Gospel to the world. According to 1 Thessalonians 3:3 & 4, all of the men knew that they were "destined" for affliction in their line of work. The missionaries' efforts were successful in the city, but some of the Jews became jealous of the great number of conversions and began stirring the town against them (cf. Acts 17:1-15). Not only did the rioters attack the house of Jason (likely one of the first Thessalonian converts), they also pursued the men as far as Berea to keep them from proclaiming the Gospel there as well (Acts 17:13). A very hostile atmosphere was looming over these new Christians' faith as God's preachers were driven out of town. These initial attacks, along with daily pressures, concerned Paul greatly and caused him to send Timothy back to Thessalonica to check on the young believers (1 Thess. 3:1-10).

WORD	GREEK-R	TRANSLITERATION	OCCURRENCES	SUGGESTED SYMBOL
Affliction	θλιβω	thlibō	4	~~Affliction~~

Marked: ☐

My Mark:

1 Thess. 1:6	received the word in much	tribulation	with the joy of the Holy Spirit,
1 Thess. 3:3	one would be disturbed by these	afflictions	; for you yourselves know that
1 Thess. 3:4	in advance that we were going to	suffer affliction	; and so it came to
1 Thess. 3:7	brethren, in all our distress and	affliction	we were comforted about you

Study:

🔍 *Tribulation* and *affliction* both come from the Greek root *thlibō* and are the most common terms in both letters to the Thessalonians that refer to persecution. Just like *faith* and *hope* have many synonyms, there are many other terms in these letters that are synonymous with *affliction*. Note the starter list below and mark these terms with a similar symbol as *affliction*. You may find other words you'll want to add, so space is provided below the list. (**Suggestion:** Look some of these words up in your Bible dictionary and compare their definitions to better understand the nature of these persecutions).

Suffered	(*paschō*)	2:2, 14
Opposition	(*agōn*)	2:2
Mistreated	(*hybrizō*)	2:2
Distress	(*anagkē*)	3:7

Marked: ☐ | **My Mark:** |

🔍 One does not have to read much of the New Testament to realize that not all people accepted the Gospel when they heard it. Thessalonica is no exception, and Paul points a finger at those who attack God's people and reject His saving message. Paul refers to this group as "the rest" (4:13) and the "others" (5:6) (Greek: *loipoi*). If you'd like, mark these terms with a distinct symbol (see "Optional Words" for a symbol suggestion). Keep this group in mind when you work through 2 Thessalonians, because there is a strong implication that these are the people who are still *afflicting* the Thessalonian Christians in 2 Thess. 1:6-10.

Marked: ☐ | **My Mark:** |

🔍 Just as you listed (and perhaps marked) the terms that described the *faith* of the Thessalonians (i.e. awake, sober, etc.), look for and list the terms that describe the "others" / "the rest" (e.g. sleep, drunk, darkness, etc.). (cf. 1 Thess. 4:13; 5:1-7).

🔍 Although the context does not necessarily suggest that the *outsiders* (*exō*) in 4:12 are persecuting the church, it may be of some interest as a term that denotes one's position in Christ. If you'd like, mark this term with another distinct symbol or the same symbol you used for *others* (*loipoi*). Cross reference 4:12 with passages like Mark 4:11 and Colossians 4:5. Write your observations below.

Marked: ☐   **My Mark:**

Question:

📖 Paul said in 2:14 that the Thessalonians imitated the churches in Judea in that they, like the Jewish Christians, suffered at the hands of their own countrymen. Recall some of the persecutions the Judean churches experienced (e.g., Hebrews 10:32-34; Acts 7:54-60; 8:1-3; 9:1-2; 12:1-3; etc.). In light of this information, how would you characterize what life might have been like for a Thessalonian Christian living in a predominantly pagan culture?

📖 What did Paul say the Jews were guilty of in their attacks against God's efforts to bring the Gospel to all the world? (cf. 2:15, 16).

📖 In what ways do Christians experience *tribulations* today? How about in your community? What about in your country?

Notes:

OPTIONAL WORDS

Optional Words are those words that are of some interest, but may not be used for a few different reasons: (1) they may not be theologically significant; (2) they may be used so frequently that to mark them would mean making your Bible pages extremely crowded or too busy to focus on the other words marked; or (3) they may just be synonyms to the key words. It will be at your discretion whether or not to mark these words. Should you choose to mark any or all of these words, a Biblical concordance can help you find their occurrences in the original language.

WORD	TRANSLITERATION	OCC...	SUGGESTED SYMBOL	MARKED
God	*theos*	37	God	☐
Lord	*kyrios*	24	Lord	☐
Jesus	*Iēsous*	16	Jesus	☐
Christ	*Christos*	10	Christ	☐
Thanks	*eucharisteō (ia)*	4	Thanks	☐
Joy	*chara*	4	Joy	☐
Rejoice	*chairō*	2	Rejoice	☐
Others	*loipoi*	2	Others	☐
Imitators	*mimētēs*	2	Imitators	☐
Example	*typos*	1	Example	☐
Satan	*Satanas*	1	Satan	☐
Unruly	*ataktos*	1	Unruly	☐

My Mark:	My Mark:
My Mark:	My Mark:
My Mark:	My Mark:
My Mark:	My Mark:
My Mark:	My Mark:
My Mark:	My Mark:

Notes:

KEY CONCLUSIONS

THEME OF 1 THESSALONIANS:

MAJOR TOPICS IN 1 THESSALONIANS:

APPLICATIONS FROM 1 THESSALONIANS:

MY KEY WORDS

If you found some words that you think are key to the text but are not listed, list them below and assign them a symbol if you wish!

WORD	CHAPTER(S)	OCCURRENCES	SYMBOL	MARKED
				☐
				☐
				☐
				☐
				☐
				☐
				☐
				☐
				☐
				☐
				☐
				☐
				☐
				☐

"Finally, brethren, pray for us that the word of the Lord will spread rapidly and be glorified, just as it did also with you;"

2 Thessalonians 3:1

2 THESSALONIANS

STUDYING 2 THESSALONIANS

1. Read the introduction to one of these guides at least once.
2. Read Acts 16:1-17:15 to understand the background of the Thessalonian church.
3. Read the "General Information" page to orient yourself to 2 Thessalonians.
4. Read 2 Thessalonians all the way through several times to familiarize yourself with the text.
5. Follow the directions found under "Key Concepts." This section will have you mark other important things prior to keywording the book.
6. Keyword the book:
    a. Turn to the first keywording page (e.g. *Faith*) and locate the suggested symbol for that particular word.
    b. Use the reference list provided in order to locate the English words in your Bible that correspond to their respective Greek word.
    c. Mark the located word with the suggested symbol. Do this for all the key words provided in each guide.
    d. When applicable, answer the questions and/or follow the study prompts included for some of the words.
    e. For an even deeper study of the word, define it using a reputable Bible dictionary.
7. Mark the optional words at your own discretion using the suggested symbols or by creating your own.
8. Complete the "Key Conclusions" section.
9. Utilize the "My Key Words" section when applicable.

GENERAL INFORMATION

AUTHOR	PAUL THE APOSTLE
GENRE	EPISTLE
DATE	c. 51 A.D.
WRITTEN FR.	CORINTH (cf. Acts 18:1-11; 2 Thess. 1:1)
RECIPIENTS	TO THE CHURCH OF THE THESSALONIANS (1:1)

Former Jews	Acts 17:1-4
God-fearing Greeks	Acts 17:4
Leading Women	Acts 17:4
Pagan Idolaters	1 Thess. 1:9

OCCASION — Paul continued to "hear" (3:11) about problems in Thessalonica even after his first letter reached the church. The apostle wrote 2 Thessalonians just a few months later to encourage the congregation in the midst of ongoing persecutions (1:3-10), to correct a misunderstanding that had developed regarding the second coming of Christ (2:1-2), and to encourage them to correct some unresolved issues among their membership (3:10-15).

KEY CONCEPTS

PURPOSE STATEMENT

Paul wants nothing more than for the Thessalonians to succeed in their new Christian lives, despite their persecutions. In so doing, they will bring glory to God and will be glorified by Him in return. This is Paul's prayer in 2 Thessalonians 1:11-12. Faithfulness at the finish line is the goal! Sometimes Paul makes very explicit statements regarding his purpose for writing (e.g., 1 Timothy 3:14-15 – "I am writing these things to you..."). However, in this case, it's a prayer. Remember that when a writer prays about something, it oftentimes reveals his primary motive for writing.

"To this end also we pray for you always, that our God will count you worthy of your calling, and fulfill every desire for goodness and the work of faith with power, so that the name of our Lord Jesus will be glorified in you, and you in Him, according to the grace of our God and the Lord Jesus Christ."
– 2 Thessalonians 1:11-12

Suggestion: Lightly underline these verses using a distinct color. (Orange?)

Marked: ☐ | **My Mark:**

Notes:

PRAYERS

Paul has prayed at least seven specific prayers for the Thessalonians between these two letters (3 in 1 Thess. & 4 in 2 Thess.). Add the prayers below to the list you began in 1 Thessalonians. Consider the relationship between all of these passionate prayers. What are some common themes Paul develops through these invocations? What seems to be heaviest on his mind while beseeching God on the Thessalonians' behalf?

Prayer for worthiness and future glory	2 Thessalonians 1:11-12
Prayer for comfort and strength	2 Thessalonians 2:16-17
Prayer for love and steadfastness	2 Thessalonians 3:5
Prayer for peace	2 Thessalonians 3:16

Suggestion: Lightly underline these prayers using a distinct color. (Purple?)

Note: 1:11-12 may already be marked as the purpose statement. You can either double up the underline (using both colors) or simply make a note in your margin that the purpose statement is also a prayer.

Marked: ☐   **My Mark:**

Notes:

PETITION VERBS

The bulk of Paul's petition verbs in this letter are used in chapter three. Notice his use of *command (parangellō)* toward the end of the letter in quick succession. Pay close attention to the matters that he is emphasizing and why. Why do you suppose Paul uses this stronger language?

PETITION VERBS	REFERENCE	GREEK	TRANSLITERATION
REQUEST	2:1	ἐρωτάω	erōtaō
EXHORT	3:12	παρακαλέω	parakaleō
COMMAND, ORDER (3:10)	3:4 3:6 3:10 3:12	παραγγέλλω	parangellō

Suggestion: Mark these words with a distinct symbol. (___↑___?)
You may also choose to underline the entire verse.

Marked: ☐   My Mark:

Notes:

THE MAN OF LAWLESSNESS

2 Thessalonians 2:1-12 ranks as one of the most difficult passages in the Bible to understand and has puzzled even the most brilliant minds of Biblical studies. Be careful as you approach this text not to superimpose any preconceived ideas of others into your study regarding who the man of lawlessness is. It may be tempting to allow that to happen, as many wild and sensational thoughts have sprung from such speculation, but you must resist! After prayer, your greatest ally for understanding is context – context – context. Remember that Paul is the one who told the Thessalonians who/what this is, not Peter, Daniel, or John, etc. Visit other places in Scripture if you must, but be sure you understand what the context of those other passages is as well before applying them to this passage. It is very tempting to offer my own opinion on this enigmatic figure, but that would be a great disservice to your exegetical journey.

In case you are unfamiliar with the popular theories concerning the identity of the man of lawlessness, the chart below has been provided to get you started. The facts of the text are listed in the left-hand column, followed by the five most prevalent theories in the subsequent columns (the seventh column is for your own use if you have another theory). Indicate in your own way (yes/no, colors, explanations, etc.) whether or not you agree if the facts of the text support a theory under its respective column. You may want to wait to engage this study until after you have keyworded the book.

Before studying 2 Thess. 2:1-12, I believe the man of lawlessness is: _____

After studying 2 Thess. 2:1-12, I believe the man of lawlessness is: _____

2 THESSALONIANS 2:1-12	SATAN	ROMAN EMPERORS	THE PAPACY	ANTICHRIST	PRINCIPLE OF EVIL	
Apostasy / falling away from the faith (Christianity) **(v. 3)**						
Yet to be revealed [c. 51 A.D.] **(vss. 3, 6 & 8)**						
Characterized by lawlessness and destined to destruction by the Lord **(vss. 3 & 8)**						
Exalts himself, sits in the temple of God, and displays himself as being God **(v. 4)**						

The Thessalonians understand who/what this is because Paul told them (v. 5)						
He is restrained, and the Thessalonians know what restrains him (vss. 6 & 7)						
Already at work [c. 51 A.D.] (v. 7)						
His restraining force will be taken out of the way (v. 7)						
He will be revealed, and then slain by the breath of the Lord (v. 8)						
His "coming" is in accord with the activity of Satan (vss. 8 & 9)						
Has power, performs signs and false wonders (v. 9)						
Deceives those who perish (v. 10)						

Study:

🔍 If you used other Scriptures to prove your answers in the chart above, keep track of them below and give your reasons for using them in this study.

Question:

📖 What/who do you believe the *man of lawlessness* is? List your main reasons below.

📖 Do you have enough information on this character to know exactly what/who this is? Would you feel comfortable teaching someone else about your findings? Why or why not?

📖 Have you ever heard someone make a very confident assertion about the identity of the man of lawlessness? What was their evidence for suggesting such? Did you accept their answer?

Notes:

KEY WORDS

BRETHREN

When the total amount of words is considered, Paul refers to the Thessalonians as *brethren* more than any other church in the New Testament. He was certainly endeared to this congregation from the very start. "Having so fond an affection for you, we were well-pleased to impart to you not only the Gospel of God but also our own lives, because you had become very dear to us" (1 Thess. 2:8). So dear in fact, that Aristarchus and Secundus of Thessalonica accompanied Paul back to Jerusalem after his third missionary journey five years later to help him deliver a contribution to the saints in Jerusalem (Acts 20:4). A few years later, we read that Aristarchus has remained with Paul through all of his trials in Jerusalem and even takes the treacherous journey to Rome with him (Acts 27:1-2). It just goes to show that there are no stronger bonds than those between Christian brothers and sisters.

WORD	GREEK-R	TRANSLITERATION	OCCURRENCES	SUGGESTED SYMBOL
Brethren	αδελφος	*adelphos*	9	Bre♥hren

Marked: ☐   **My Mark:**

2 Thess. 1:3	to give thanks to God for you,	brethren	, as is *only* fitting, because your
2 Thess. 2:1	Now we request you,	brethren	, with regard to the coming of our
2 Thess. 2:13	give thanks to God for you,	brethren	beloved by the Lord, because God
2 Thess. 2:15	So then,	brethren	, stand firm and hold to the
2 Thess. 3:1	Finally,	brethren	, pray for us that the word of the
2 Thess. 3:6	Now we command you,	brethren	, in the name of our Lord Jesus
2 Thess. 3:6	that you keep away from every	brother	who leads an unruly life and not
2 Thess. 3:13	But as for you,	brethren	, do not grow weary of doing good.
2 Thess. 3:15	an enemy, but admonish him as a	brother	.

Study:

🔍 Just as you marked *imitators* (*mimētēs*) in 1 Thessalonians, the same word should be found and marked in this second letter. Here, *mimētēs* is translated twice in 2 Thessalonians as *example* – (3:7, 9). (See "Optional Words" for a symbol suggestion). Also note the word, *model* (*typos*) in 2 Thess. 3:9. Mark it the same way you marked *typos* in 1 Thessalonians.

Marked: ☐   **My Mark:**

🔍 Recall that Paul had instructed the leadership in Thessalonica to admonish the *unruly* among them in 1 Thessalonians 5:14. Apparently things had not improved with this wayward group of slothful Christians in the time it took for Paul to write to them a second time. If you'd like, locate and mark *unruly / undisciplined* (R – *tassō*) in 3:6, 7, & 11. (See "Optional Words" for a symbol suggestion).

Marked: ☐ | **My Mark:**

🔍 The root form of *unruly* (*tassō*) was mentioned here because Paul uses a different lemma form of the word in 3:7 (*atakteō* [verb], rather than *ataktos* [adverb]). These words are very similar in definition, but there are some noteworthy differences in their uses. Use a Bible dictionary to define these two words and note any differences you find.

Definition of *atakteō*:

_____

_____

Definition of *ataktos*:

_____

Question:

📖 Based on the definitions of the 'unruly' terms above and the contexts of the passages, how would you describe the actions of these *unruly* Christians in your own words?

_____

_____

📖 How are the Thessalonians supposed to handle these *undisciplined* individuals? (Cf. 1 Thess. 5:12-15; 2 Thess. 3:14-15)

_____

_____

📖 Do you think it's easier or harder to encourage and instruct people that are your spiritual brothers and sisters? Why?

_____

_____

Notes:

LOVE

Just like in Paul's first letter, *brethren* and *love* are two recurring key words in this second letter that strike at the core of Christian relationship. Five occurrences may not seem like much, but in a short three-chapter book that is the sequel to 1 Thessalonians which contained words like: *brethren, encourage, one another, love, thanks, joy,* etc. this word deserves a spot toward the top. Notice that since Paul wrote to them last, their "faith is greatly enlarged," and their "*love*...toward one another grows ever greater" (2 Thess. 1:3). Every good thing about this congregation seems to only get better. These Christians stand in direct contrast to those who did not "receive the *love* of the truth" (2:10) and have only increased in their "*love* of God" (3:5). There was no mistaking this church body for any other human organization. Jesus Himself said, "By this all men will know that you are My disciples, if you have *love* for one another" (John 13:35).

WORD	GREEK-R	TRANSLITERATION	OCCURRENCES	SUGGESTED SYMBOL
Love	αγαπαω	*agapaō*	5	L♥ve

Marked: ☐   **My Mark:**

2 Thess. 1:3	is greatly enlarged, and the	love	of each one of you toward one
2 Thess. 2:10	because they did not receive the	love	of the truth so as to be saved.
2 Thess. 2:13	thanks to God for you, brethren	beloved	by the Lord, because God has
2 Thess. 2:16	and God our Father, who has	loved	us and given us eternal comfort
2 Thess. 3:5	Lord direct your hearts into the	love	of God and into the steadfastness

Question:

📖 What do you think Paul's main goals are when he writes to the Thessalonians about *love*? Compare your notes to your observations on *love* from 1 Thessalonians.

📖 Consider the varied demographics of the church in Thessalonica and the external pressures they were experiencing. How do you think this congregation developed a "greatly enlarged" *love* for each other?

📖 What things make it hard for you to *love* your brothers/sisters in Christ? How do you overcome those obstacles?

📖 Regarding the lives of the Thessalonians and their *love* for one another, what other applications do you see for Christians today?

Notes:

FAITH

Whatever persecutions and pressures the Thessalonians may have faced since the time Paul wrote to them last were apparently not enough to shake them. In fact, Paul immediately commends them because their faith is absolutely flourishing despite others' attempted hindrances, saying in 1:3, "...your faith is greatly enlarged." Who would have thought that if a congregation obeyed the Lord's commands, relied on one another, prayed, etc. that they would be doing well? They continue to own their faith day by day, essentially becoming the model young church. Beaming with pride, Paul tells them in 1:4 that "we ourselves speak proudly of you among the churches of God for your perseverance and faith in the midst of all your persecutions and afflictions which you endure."

WORD	GREEK-R	TRANSLITERATION	OCCURRENCES	SUGGESTED SYMBOL
Faith	πιστευω	*pisteuō*	10	Faith

Marked: ☐   **My Mark:**

2 Thess. 1:3	as is *only* fitting, because your	faith	is greatly enlarged, and the love
2 Thess. 1:4	for your perseverance and	faith	in the midst of all your
2 Thess. 1:10	marveled at among all who have	believed	—for our testimony to you was
2 Thess. 1:10	for our testimony to you was	believed	.
2 Thess. 1:11	for goodness and the work of	faith	with power,
2 Thess. 2:11	influence so that they will	believe	what is false,
2 Thess. 2:12	all may be judged who did not	believe	the truth, but took pleasure in
2 Thess. 2:13	sanctification by the Spirit and	faith	in the truth.
2 Thess. 3:2	and evil men; for not all have	faith	.
2 Thess. 3:3	But the Lord is	faithful	, and He will strengthen and

WORD	GREEK-R	TRANSLITERATION	OCCURRENCES	SUGGESTED SYMBOL
Hope	ελπις	*elpis*	1	Hope

Marked: ☐   **My Mark:**

| 2 Thess. 2:16 | given us eternal comfort and good | hope | by grace, |

Study:

🔍 Revisit the list of 'faith words' in the Faith study section of 1 Thessalonians (Pg. 32) and recall all the terms Paul used to solidify this congregation's faith. These Christians have done wonderfully, warding off several threats to their convictions. However, more threats are seeking a way in – and Paul knows it. Just like you did for 1 Thessalonians, look for other synonyms that compliment *faith* (*pisteuō*) and *hope* (*elpis*) and mark them in a distinctive way. (**Suggestion:** Put a green box around these words and phrases).

Endure	(*anechomai*)	1:4
Steadfastness	(*hupomonē*)	1:4 (perseverance); 3:5
Stand Firm	(*stēkō*)	2:15
Hold	(*krateō*)	2:15
Comfort	(*paraklēsis*)	2:16
	(*parakaleō*)	2:17
Strengthen	(*stērizō*)	2:17; 3:3
Protect	(*phulassō*)	3:3
"Do not grow weary"		3:13

Marked: ☐   **My Mark:**

Question:

📖 What do you notice about the church in Thessalonica that kept them strong and ready to deflect attacks on their *faith*? Which of these qualities do you need to implement in your own walk of faith?

📖 When comparing 1 and 2 Thessalonians, what do you notice about the Lord and His faithfulness? In practicality, what does it mean that the Lord is faithful?

📖 Paul commends the Thessalonians in 1:3 because their "faith is greatly enlarged." What does a greatly enlarged faith look like for a Christian?

📖 Is a growing faith measurable? Or is it more ambiguous …"you'll know it when you see it"? Is *your* faith growing? How can you tell?

Notes:

GLORY

Why put away worthless idols to serve a living God? To gain the *glory*. Why endure suffering and afflictions at the hands of nonbelievers for your faith? To gain the *glory* – the *glory* of our Lord Jesus Christ (2:14). The root word for *glory*, *dokeō*, is used by Paul seven times in his second letter to these Christians. Compare this to the fact that the root word, *dokeō*, occurs only five times in 1 Thessalonians, with only one reference having much to do with the glory of God. In a concerted effort to encourage this group, Paul seems to have doubled down on his emphasis of the reward for faithful believers. Trials and tribulations will be worth it. Living holy in a Godless community that attacks you for your beliefs will be worth it. Glorifying God in this life and gaining His eternal glory hereafter will be worth anything this life has to throw at us (cf. Rom. 8:17-18; Phil. 3:20-21).

WORD	GREEK-R	TRANSLITERATION	OCCURRENCES	SUGGESTED SYMBOL
Glory	δοκεω	*dokeō*	7	Glory

Marked: ☐   **My Mark:**

2 Thess. 1:9	presence of the Lord and from the	glory	of His power,
2 Thess. 1:10	when He comes to	be glorified	in His saints on that
2 Thess. 1:11	your calling, and fulfill every	desire	for goodness and the work of
2 Thess. 1:12	the name of our Lord Jesus will	be glorified	in you, and you in Him,
2 Thess. 2:12	did not believe the truth, but	took pleasure	in wickedness.
2 Thess. 2:14	our gospel, that you may gain the	glory	of our Lord Jesus Christ.
2 Thess. 3:1	Lord will spread rapidly and be	glorified	, just *as it* did also with you;

Study:

🔍 *Dokeō* is translated as *glory* in 1 Thessalonians 2:6, 12, & 20. If you would like, mark those occurrences with the same symbol as well.

Marked: ☐   **My Mark:**

🔍 A noteworthy word that you may have already identified and listed in 1 Thessalonians under the key word, *holy*, is that of *worthy* (*axiōs*) (cf. 1 Thess. 2:12). If you'd like, mark *worthy* with a distinct symbol in 2 Thessalonians 1:5 & 11 (see "Optional Words" for a symbol suggestion).

Marked: ☐   **My Mark:**

Question:

📖 How would you define what the *glory* of Christ is?

📖 According to 2:14, how does one gain the *glory* of Jesus Christ?

📖 The phrase "took pleasure in wickedness" in 2 Thessalonians 2:12 may be translated as "gloried in wickedness." What do you suppose that means? Do people still do this today?

Notes:

WORD

During the months between Paul's first and second letters to Thessalonica, it appears that some devious individuals began disturbing the church with false statements. Paul is quick to remind them of the things he spoke to them in person and urges them to disregard any information that contradicts what he taught them. Even if someone seems to have an inspired letter, or convincing, prophetic message, it must be compared to what an actual apostle taught them before receiving it (2 Thess. 2:1-3; cf. 1 Thess. 5:19-22). Remember that Paul's message – the Gospel – came directly from Jesus Himself (Galatians 1:11, 12) and, he, in turn imparted it to the Thessalonians with power, conviction, and the Holy Spirit (1 Thess. 1:5). Paul also calls their attention to the fact that his letters have a distinguishing mark (2 Thess. 3:17), which proves it is him writing and not another so-called apostle. The word, *tradition* (*paradosis*) has been included in this section since it is complimentary to God's *Word* and the term, *Gospel*.

WORD	GREEK-R	TRANSLITERATION	OCCURRENCES	SUGGESTED SYMBOL
Word	λεγω	*legō*	7	◁Word◁

Marked: ☐   **My Mark:**

2 Thess. 2:2	disturbed either by a spirit or a	message	or a letter as if from us, to the
2 Thess. 2:4	and exalts himself above every	so-called	god or object of worship, so that
2 Thess. 2:5	while I was still with you, I was	telling	you these things?
2 Thess. 2:15	you were taught, whether by	word	*of mouth* or by letter from us.
2 Thess. 2:17	hearts in every good work and	word	.
2 Thess. 3:1	brethren, pray for us that the	word	of the Lord will spread rapidly
2 Thess. 3:14	If anyone does not obey our	instruction	in this letter, take special note

WORD	GREEK-R	TRANSLITERATION	OCCURRENCES	SUGGESTED SYMBOL
Gospel	ευαγγελιον	*euaggelion*	2	◁Gospel◁

Marked: ☐   **My Mark:**

2 Thess. 1:8	those who do not obey the	gospel	of our Lord Jesus.
2 Thess. 2:14	He called you through our	gospel	, that you may gain the glory of

WORD	GREEK-L	TRANSLITERATION	OCCURRENCES	SUGGESTED SYMBOL
Tradition	παράδοσις	*paradosis*	2	Tradition

Marked: ☐   **My Mark:**

2 Thess. 2:15	stand firm and hold to the	traditions	which you were taught, whether by
2 Thess. 3:6	life and not according to the	tradition	which you received from us.

Study:

- Even though *traditions* (*paradosis*) is only used twice in this letter, it has great significance. *Traditions* refer to those beliefs and practices that have been passed down. Paul passed down what he received from the Lord (cf. Galatians 1:11-12) and the Thessalonians in turn passed on what they received from an apostle to others (cf. 1 Thess. 1:8). If you'd like, define this word using your Bible dictionary and record it below to have it ready when answering some of the discussion questions in this section.

  Definition of *traditions* (*paradosis*):

  _____

  _____

- Since you marked *received* in 1 Thessalonians, mark *received* in 2 Thessalonians 2:10 and 3:6 with the same symbol. Make note of the things both *received* and **not** *received* in these passages and the ones in 1 Thessalonians. Compare the two.

  _____

  _____

Marked: ☐   **My Mark:**

Question:

- 📖 According to 2:15, what methods of communication from inspired individuals did Paul consider authoritative? How does the word, *traditions*, teach us where our authority comes from today for doing what we do as Christians?

  _____

  _____

📖 How has the concept of *tradition* been utilized by people through the ages to either modify or totally replace apostolic teachings and patterns? (cf. Mark 7:1-13)

📖 What else is interesting about the way Paul uses the term, *word* (*legō*)?

Notes:

WORK

Every dynamic of *working* and *laboring* that Paul discussed in 1 Thessalonians is seen again in his second letter and then some. The Thessalonians are still striving in their *work* of faith (1:11) and trying to follow Paul's example of working hard daily to provide for themselves. However, some among them are still not pulling their weight, doing no work and acting like busybodies (3:10-12). Paul pulls no punches in chapter three as he explains what will become of lazy people who are unwilling to work. The new dimension of *working* that is not seen in 1 Thessalonians is that of the "man of lawlessness" in chapter two. Three of the ten uses of *work* (ergon) in this letter are found in the section describing the activities of this enigmatic figure. Before jumping to conclusions in this section, remember to work through the chart about this character under "Key Concepts."

WORD	GREEK-R	TRANSLITERATION	OCCURRENCES	SUGGESTED SYMBOL
Work	εργον	*ergon*	10	Work

Marked: ☐   **My Mark:**

2 Thess. 1:11	desire for goodness and the	work	of faith with power,
2 Thess. 2:7	mystery of lawlessness is already at	work	; only he who now
2 Thess. 2:9	coming is in accord with the	activity	of Satan, with all power and signs
2 Thess. 2:11	will send upon them a deluding	influence	so that they will believe what is
2 Thess. 2:17	your hearts in every good	work	and word.
2 Thess. 3:8	labor and hardship we *kept*	working	night and day so that we would
2 Thess. 3:10	if anyone is not willing to	work	, then he is not to eat, either.
2 Thess. 3:11	an undisciplined life, doing no	work	at all, but acting like
2 Thess. 3:11	life, doing no work at all, but	acting	like busybodies.
2 Thess. 3:12	in the Lord Jesus Christ to	work	in quiet fashion and eat their own

Study:

🔍 Mark the word *labor* in 2 Thessalonians 3:8 the same way you did in 1 Thessalonians. Remember that *labor* and *work* are contextually related. You may also want to mark *hardship* in the same verse with the symbol you used in 1 Thessalonians. Refer to your definitions of these words in 1 Thessalonians for a refresher, if needed (Pg. 50).

Marked: ☐   **My Mark:**

🔍 Categorize the different ways that Paul uses the term *work*. It might be helpful to make a separate list for each type of use. Some starter categories have been provided below. Add your own as you see fit. **Note:** You may want to incorporate your observations from *Work* in 1 Thessalonians.

Spiritual works of the Thessalonians:

Paul's instructions and personal example regarding physical work:

Works of the man of lawlessness as seen in the text:

_____:

Question:

📖 Have you ever found yourself in a situation like the one Paul describes in 3:6-15? What did that look like and how did you handle it?

📖 How else does Paul characterize those who are unwilling to work?

📖 How does God require a faithful child of His to work? Would you say that you are working in the ways God desires? Why or why not?

Notes:

AFFLICTION

Persecutions and hardships have not eased for the Thessalonians since the first time Paul wrote them. Although they are doing well and their faith is still growing, Paul continues to encourage them and give them hope that they are doing what is right and that their endurance will be worth it. The apostle assures them that God is on their side and does indeed take it personally when His people are attacked. "For after all it is only just for God to repay with affliction those who afflict you" (2 Thess. 1:6). Paul probably remembers the very words the Lord spoke to him from Heaven when he was persecuting the church in Acts 9:4 – "Saul, Saul, why are you persecuting Me?" If you are an enemy of God's people, then you are an enemy of God Himself. Genuine Christianity may not be easy, but it is right. On the verge of execution, Paul reflected upon his sufferings for the Gospel years later in 2 Timothy 3:12, and stated what all Christians either know or will come to know: "Indeed, all who desire to live godly in Christ Jesus will be persecuted."

WORD	GREEK-R	TRANSLITERATION	OCCURRENCES	SUGGESTED SYMBOL
Affliction	θλίβω	*thlibō*	4	~~Affliction~~

Marked: ☐   **My Mark:**

2 Thess. 1:4	of all your persecutions and	afflictions	which you endure.
2 Thess. 1:6	*only* just for God to repay with	affliction	those who afflict you,
2 Thess. 1:6	repay with affliction those who	afflict	you,
2 Thess. 1:7	and *to give* relief to you who are	afflicted	and to us as well when the Lord

Study:

🔍 You have already marked several words in 1 Thessalonians that are closely related to *affliction* (i.e., suffering, opposition, etc.). *Suffering* (*paschō*) occurs in 2 Thessalonians 1:5 if you'd like to mark it. You may also want to mark *persecutions* (*diōgmos*) in 1:4 with a similar symbol. If you defined the 'affliction words' under the *affliction* section in 1 Thessalonians, add *persecutions* (*diōgmos*) to your list.

Marked: ☐   **My Mark:**

🔍 Recall Paul's references to "the rest" and the "others" in 1 Thessalonians. Compare what you know about those individuals with those who are said to be afflicting the Thessalonians in 2 Thess. 1:6-10. List the differences and similarities between these people. Do you think it's the same group(s)?

🔍 If you already marked *Satan, tempter,* and *tempted* in 1 Thessalonians and want to keep track of references to Satan, you may want to mark *Satan* in 2 Thessalonians 2:9 and "the evil one" in 3:3 with the same symbol.

Marked: ☐ | **My Mark:**

Question:

📖 According to Paul, what will be the result of the Thessalonians' *afflictions* if they endure?

📖 What will be the outcome for those who are *afflicting* this church? What are some other reasons the Lord will "deal out retribution" to those individuals? (c.f. 1:8)

📖 Regarding *affliction* in 1 Thessalonians, you listed some ways in which Christians in general experience tribulations today. Are you experiencing hardships because of your own faith? Why or why not?

Notes:

OPTIONAL WORDS

WORD	TRANSLITERATION	OCC...	SUGGESTED SYMBOL	MARKED
Lord	*kurios*	22	Lord (▽)	☐
God	*theos*	18	God (△)	☐
Jesus	*Iēsous*	13	Jesus (✝)	☐
Christ	*Christos*	10	Christ	☐
Unruly	*tassō*	3	Unruly	☐
Worthy	*axios*	2	Worthy	☐
Example	*mimētēs*	2	(Example)	☐
Model	*typos*	1	(Model)	☐

My Mark:

My Mark:

My Mark:

My Mark:

My Mark:

My Mark:

My Mark:

My Mark:

Notes:

KEY CONCLUSIONS

THEME OF 2 THESSALONIANS:

MAJOR TOPICS IN 2 THESSALONIANS:

APPLICATIONS FROM 2 THESSALONIANS:

MY KEY WORDS

WORD	CHAPTER(S)	OCCURRENCES	SYMBOL	MARKED
				☐
				☐
				☐
				☐
				☐
				☐
				☐
				☐
				☐
				☐
				☐
				☐
				☐
				☐

www.ingramcontent.com/pod-product-compliance
Lightning Source LLC
Chambersburg PA
CBHW081500070526
44586CB00019B/2436